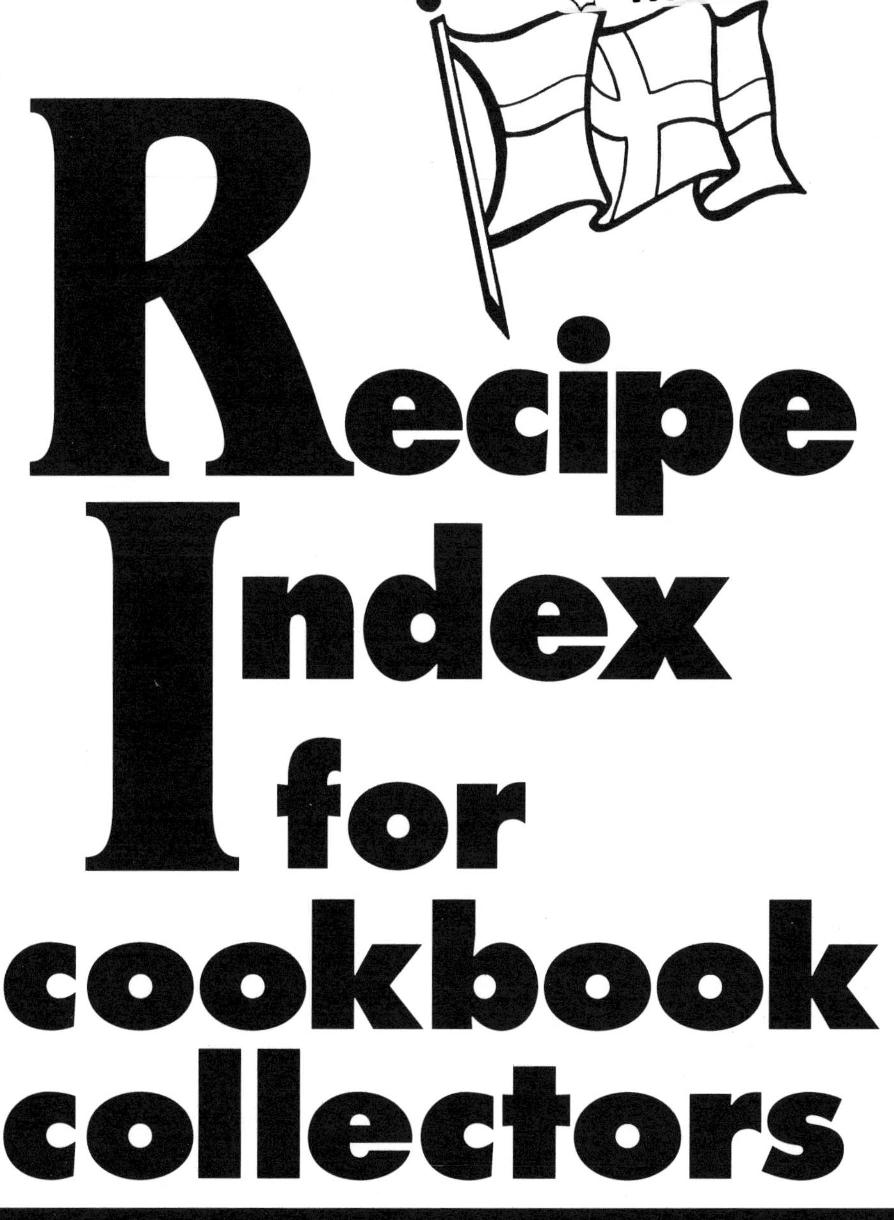

# Recipe Index for cookbook collectors

*...Finally, at your fingertips...*

**Your favorite recipes from your cookbook collection!**

*By Maria Baker*

Also by Maria Baker
"Yes, You May Have The Recipe"
Cookbook

"Potpourri of Recipes"
All Occasion Recipe Booklet Cards

"Recipes from our Family Tree"
Gift Book

Cover Design and Illustrations
By William Collier, Lake Forest, IL

Printed in United States of America
By Glenbard Graphics, Carol Stream, IL 60188



ISBN Number 0-9620102-3-5

# INTRODUCTION

RECIPE INDEX FOR COOKBOOK COLLECTORS is a book to help you FIND THE RECIPE you want WHEN YOU WANT IT.

Finally an end to the frustration of searching through your cookbook collection, page after page, trying to find that special recipe you want to try, *now.*

When you prepare that special recipe, record the title in the proper category, the title of the cookbook and the page it is on.

THE END OF FRUSTRATION!

# CONTENTS

# BEVERAGES

Recipe Name

Cookbook | Page

Recipe Name

Cookbook | Page

Recipe Name

Cookbook | Page

Recipe Name

Cookbook | Page

Recipe Name

Cookbook | Page

Recipe Name

Cookbook | Page

Recipe Name

Cookbook | Page

Recipe Name

Cookbook | Page

Recipe Name

Cookbook | Page

Recipe Name

Cookbook | Page

Recipe Name

Cookbook | Page

Recipe Name

Cookbook | Page

Recipe Name

Cookbook | Page

**Recipe Index**

Recipe Name

Cookbook | Page

Recipe Name

Cookbook | Page

Recipe Name

Cookbook | Page

Recipe Name

Cookbook | Page

Recipe Name

Cookbook | Page

Recipe Name

Cookbook | Page

Recipe Name

Cookbook | Page

Recipe Name

Cookbook | Page

Recipe Name

Cookbook | Page

Recipe Name

Cookbook | Page

Recipe Name

Cookbook | Page

Recipe Name

Cookbook | Page

Recipe Name

Cookbook | Page

Recipe Name

Cookbook | Page

Recipe Name

Cookbook | Page

Recipe Name

Cookbook | Page

Recipe Name

Cookbook | Page

Recipe Name

Cookbook | Page

Recipe Name

Cookbook | Page

Recipe Name

Cookbook | Page

Recipe Name

Cookbook | Page

Recipe Name

Cookbook | Page

Recipe Name

Cookbook | Page

Recipe Name

Cookbook | Page

Recipe Name

Cookbook | Page

Recipe Name

Cookbook | Page

**Recipe Index**

Recipe Name

Cookbook | Page

Recipe Name

Cookbook | Page

Recipe Name

Cookbook | Page

Recipe Name

Cookbook | Page

Recipe Name

Cookbook | Page

Recipe Name

Cookbook | Page

Recipe Name

Cookbook | Page

Recipe Name

Cookbook | Page

Recipe Name

Cookbook | Page

Recipe Name

Cookbook | Page

Recipe Name

Cookbook | Page

Recipe Name

Cookbook | Page

Recipe Name

Cookbook | Page

# APPETIZERS

Recipe Name
Cookbook | Page

Recipe Name
Cookbook | Page

Recipe Name
Cookbook | Page

Recipe Name
Cookbook | Page

Recipe Name
Cookbook | Page

Recipe Name
Cookbook | Page

Recipe Name
Cookbook | Page

Recipe Name
Cookbook | Page

Recipe Name
Cookbook | Page

Recipe Name
Cookbook | Page

Recipe Name
Cookbook | Page

Recipe Name
Cookbook | Page

Recipe Name
Cookbook | Page

**Recipe Index**

Recipe Name

Cookbook | Page

Recipe Name

Cookbook | Page

Recipe Name

Cookbook | Page

Recipe Name

Cookbook | Page

Recipe Name

Cookbook | Page

Recipe Name

Cookbook | Page

Recipe Name

Cookbook | Page

Recipe Name

Cookbook | Page

Recipe Name

Cookbook | Page

Recipe Name

Cookbook | Page

Recipe Name

Cookbook | Page

Recipe Name

Cookbook | Page

Recipe Name

Cookbook | Page

Recipe Name

Cookbook | Page

Recipe Name

Cookbook | Page

Recipe Name

Cookbook | Page

Recipe Name

Cookbook | Page

Recipe Name

Cookbook | Page

Recipe Name

Cookbook | Page

Recipe Name

Cookbook | Page

Recipe Name

Cookbook | Page

Recipe Name

Cookbook | Page

Recipe Name

Cookbook | Page

Recipe Name

Cookbook | Page

Recipe Name

Cookbook | Page

Recipe Name

Cookbook | Page

**Recipe Index**

Recipe Name
Cookbook | Page

Recipe Name
Cookbook | Page

Recipe Name
Cookbook | Page

Recipe Name
Cookbook | Page

Recipe Name
Cookbook | Page

Recipe Name
Cookbook | Page

Recipe Name
Cookbook | Page

Recipe Name
Cookbook | Page

Recipe Name
Cookbook | Page

Recipe Name
Cookbook | Page

Recipe Name
Cookbook | Page

Recipe Name
Cookbook | Page

Recipe Name
Cookbook | Page

Recipe Name

Cookbook | Page

Recipe Name

Cookbook | Page

Recipe Name

Cookbook | Page

Recipe Name

Cookbook | Page

Recipe Name

Cookbook | Page

Recipe Name

Cookbook | Page

Recipe Name

Cookbook | Page

Recipe Name

Cookbook | Page

Recipe Name

Cookbook | Page

Recipe Name

Cookbook | Page

Recipe Name

Cookbook | Page

Recipe Name

Cookbook | Page

Recipe Name

Cookbook | Page

## Recipe Index

Recipe Name

Cookbook | Page

Recipe Name

Cookbook | Page

Recipe Name

Cookbook | Page

Recipe Name

Cookbook | Page

Recipe Name

Cookbook | Page

Recipe Name

Cookbook | Page

Recipe Name

Cookbook | Page

Recipe Name

Cookbook | Page

Recipe Name

Cookbook | Page

Recipe Name

Cookbook | Page

Recipe Name

Cookbook | Page

Recipe Name

Cookbook | Page

Recipe Name

Cookbook | Page

Recipe Name

Cookbook | Page

Recipe Name

Cookbook | Page

Recipe Name

Cookbook | Page

Recipe Name

Cookbook | Page

Recipe Name

Cookbook | Page

Recipe Name

Cookbook | Page

Recipe Name

Cookbook | Page

Recipe Name

Cookbook | Page

Recipe Name

Cookbook | Page

Recipe Name

Cookbook | Page

Recipe Name

Cookbook | Page

Recipe Name

Cookbook | Page

Recipe Name

Cookbook | Page

**Recipe Index**

Recipe Name

Cookbook | Page

Recipe Name

Cookbook | Page

Recipe Name

Cookbook | Page

Recipe Name

Cookbook | Page

Recipe Name

Cookbook | Page

Recipe Name

Cookbook | Page

Recipe Name

Cookbook | Page

Recipe Name

Cookbook | Page

Recipe Name

Cookbook | Page

Recipe Name

Cookbook | Page

Recipe Name

Cookbook | Page

Recipe Name

Cookbook | Page

Recipe Name

Cookbook | Page

# BREADS

Recipe Name

Cookbook | Page

Recipe Name

Cookbook | Page

Recipe Name

Cookbook | Page

Recipe Name

Cookbook | Page

Recipe Name

Cookbook | Page

Recipe Name

Cookbook | Page

Recipe Name

Cookbook | Page

Recipe Name

Cookbook | Page

Recipe Name

Cookbook | Page

Recipe Name

Cookbook | Page

Recipe Name

Cookbook | Page

Recipe Name

Cookbook | Page

Recipe Name

Cookbook | Page

**Recipe Index**

Recipe Name

Cookbook | Page

Recipe Name

Cookbook | Page

Recipe Name

Cookbook | Page

Recipe Name

Cookbook | Page

Recipe Name

Cookbook | Page

Recipe Name

Cookbook | Page

Recipe Name

Cookbook | Page

Recipe Name

Cookbook | Page

Recipe Name

Cookbook | Page

Recipe Name

Cookbook | Page

Recipe Name

Cookbook | Page

Recipe Name

Cookbook | Page

Recipe Name

Cookbook | Page

Recipe Name

Cookbook | Page

Recipe Name

Cookbook | Page

Recipe Name

Cookbook | Page

Recipe Name

Cookbook | Page

Recipe Name

Cookbook | Page

Recipe Name

Cookbook | Page

Recipe Name

Cookbook | Page

Recipe Name

Cookbook | Page

Recipe Name

Cookbook | Page

Recipe Name

Cookbook | Page

Recipe Name

Cookbook | Page

Recipe Name

Cookbook | Page

Recipe Name

Cookbook | Page

**Recipe Index**

Recipe Name

Cookbook | Page

Recipe Name

Cookbook | Page

Recipe Name

Cookbook | Page

Recipe Name

Cookbook | Page

Recipe Name

Cookbook | Page

Recipe Name

Cookbook | Page

Recipe Name

Cookbook | Page

Recipe Name

Cookbook | Page

Recipe Name

Cookbook | Page

Recipe Name

Cookbook | Page

Recipe Name

Cookbook | Page

Recipe Name

Cookbook | Page

Recipe Name

Cookbook | Page

Recipe Name

Cookbook | Page

Recipe Name

Cookbook | Page

Recipe Name

Cookbook | Page

Recipe Name

Cookbook | Page

Recipe Name

Cookbook | Page

Recipe Name

Cookbook | Page

Recipe Name

Cookbook | Page

Recipe Name

Cookbook | Page

Recipe Name

Cookbook | Page

Recipe Name

Cookbook | Page

Recipe Name

Cookbook | Page

Recipe Name

Cookbook | Page

Recipe Name

Cookbook | Page

**Recipe Index**

Recipe Name

Cookbook | Page

Recipe Name

Cookbook | Page

Recipe Name

Cookbook | Page

Recipe Name

Cookbook | Page

Recipe Name

Cookbook | Page

Recipe Name

Cookbook | Page

Recipe Name

Cookbook | Page

Recipe Name

Cookbook | Page

Recipe Name

Cookbook | Page

Recipe Name

Cookbook | Page

Recipe Name

Cookbook | Page

Recipe Name

Cookbook | Page

Recipe Name

Cookbook | Page

Recipe Name

Cookbook | Page

Recipe Name

Cookbook | Page

Recipe Name

Cookbook | Page

Recipe Name

Cookbook | Page

Recipe Name

Cookbook | Page

Recipe Name

Cookbook | Page

Recipe Name

Cookbook | Page

Recipe Name

Cookbook | Page

Recipe Name

Cookbook | Page

Recipe Name

Cookbook | Page

Recipe Name

Cookbook | Page

Recipe Name

Cookbook | Page

Recipe Name

Cookbook | Page

## Recipe Index

Recipe Name

| Cookbook | Page |
|---|---|

Recipe Name

| Cookbook | Page |
|---|---|

Recipe Name

| Cookbook | Page |
|---|---|

Recipe Name

| Cookbook | Page |
|---|---|

Recipe Name

| Cookbook | Page |
|---|---|

Recipe Name

| Cookbook | Page |
|---|---|

Recipe Name

| Cookbook | Page |
|---|---|

Recipe Name

| Cookbook | Page |
|---|---|

Recipe Name

| Cookbook | Page |
|---|---|

Recipe Name

| Cookbook | Page |
|---|---|

Recipe Name

| Cookbook | Page |
|---|---|

Recipe Name

| Cookbook | Page |
|---|---|

Recipe Name

| Cookbook | Page |
|---|---|

# PANCAKES and WAFFLES

Recipe Name

Cookbook | Page

Recipe Name

Cookbook | Page

Recipe Name

Cookbook | Page

Recipe Name

Cookbook | Page

Recipe Name

Cookbook | Page

Recipe Name

Cookbook | Page

Recipe Name

Cookbook | Page

Recipe Name

Cookbook | Page

Recipe Name

Cookbook | Page

Recipe Name

Cookbook | Page

Recipe Name

Cookbook | Page

Recipe Name

Cookbook | Page

Recipe Name

Cookbook | Page

**Recipe Index**

Recipe Name
Cookbook | Page

Recipe Name
Cookbook | Page

Recipe Name
Cookbook | Page

Recipe Name
Cookbook | Page

Recipe Name
Cookbook | Page

Recipe Name
Cookbook | Page

Recipe Name
Cookbook | Page

Recipe Name
Cookbook | Page

Recipe Name
Cookbook | Page

Recipe Name
Cookbook | Page

Recipe Name
Cookbook | Page

Recipe Name
Cookbook | Page

Recipe Name
Cookbook | Page

# EGGS and CHEESE

Recipe Name

Cookbook | Page

Recipe Name

Cookbook | Page

Recipe Name

Cookbook | Page

Recipe Name

Cookbook | Page

Recipe Name

Cookbook | Page

Recipe Name

Cookbook | Page

Recipe Name

Cookbook | Page

Recipe Name

Cookbook | Page

Recipe Name

Cookbook | Page

Recipe Name

Cookbook | Page

Recipe Name

Cookbook | Page

Recipe Name

Cookbook | Page

Recipe Name

Cookbook | Page

## Recipe Index

| Recipe Name | |
|---|---|
| Cookbook | Page |
| Recipe Name | |
| Cookbook | Page |
| Recipe Name | |
| Cookbook | Page |
| Recipe Name | |
| Cookbook | Page |
| Recipe Name | |
| Cookbook | Page |
| Recipe Name | |
| Cookbook | Page |
| Recipe Name | |
| Cookbook | Page |
| Recipe Name | |
| Cookbook | Page |
| Recipe Name | |
| Cookbook | Page |
| Recipe Name | |
| Cookbook | Page |
| Recipe Name | |
| Cookbook | Page |
| Recipe Name | |
| Cookbook | Page |
| Recipe Name | |
| Cookbook | Page |

# SOUPS, SANDWICHES and SAUCES

Recipe Name

Cookbook | Page

Recipe Name

Cookbook | Page

Recipe Name

Cookbook | Page

Recipe Name

Cookbook | Page

Recipe Name

Cookbook | Page

Recipe Name

Cookbook | Page

Recipe Name

Cookbook | Page

Recipe Name

Cookbook | Page

Recipe Name

Cookbook | Page

Recipe Name

Cookbook | Page

Recipe Name

Cookbook | Page

Recipe Name

Cookbook | Page

Recipe Name

Cookbook | Page

**Recipe Index**

Recipe Name

Cookbook | Page

Recipe Name

Cookbook | Page

Recipe Name

Cookbook | Page

Recipe Name

Cookbook | Page

Recipe Name

Cookbook | Page

Recipe Name

Cookbook | Page

Recipe Name

Cookbook | Page

Recipe Name

Cookbook | Page

Recipe Name

Cookbook | Page

Recipe Name

Cookbook | Page

Recipe Name

Cookbook | Page

Recipe Name

Cookbook | Page

Recipe Name

Cookbook | Page

Recipe Name

Cookbook | Page

Recipe Name

Cookbook | Page

Recipe Name

Cookbook | Page

Recipe Name

Cookbook | Page

Recipe Name

Cookbook | Page

Recipe Name

Cookbook | Page

Recipe Name

Cookbook | Page

Recipe Name

Cookbook | Page

Recipe Name

Cookbook | Page

Recipe Name

Cookbook | Page

Recipe Name

Cookbook | Page

Recipe Name

Cookbook | Page

Recipe Name

Cookbook | Page

**Recipe Index**

Recipe Name

Cookbook | Page

Recipe Name

Cookbook | Page

Recipe Name

Cookbook | Page

Recipe Name

Cookbook | Page

Recipe Name

Cookbook | Page

Recipe Name

Cookbook | Page

Recipe Name

Cookbook | Page

Recipe Name

Cookbook | Page

Recipe Name

Cookbook | Page

Recipe Name

Cookbook | Page

Recipe Name

Cookbook | Page

Recipe Name

Cookbook | Page

Recipe Name

Cookbook | Page

Recipe Name

Cookbook | Page

Recipe Name

Cookbook | Page

Recipe Name

Cookbook | Page

Recipe Name

Cookbook | Page

Recipe Name

Cookbook | Page

Recipe Name

Cookbook | Page

Recipe Name

Cookbook | Page

Recipe Name

Cookbook | Page

Recipe Name

Cookbook | Page

Recipe Name

Cookbook | Page

Recipe Name

Cookbook | Page

Recipe Name

Cookbook | Page

Recipe Name

Cookbook | Page

**Recipe Index**

Recipe Name

Cookbook Page

Recipe Name

Cookbook Page

Recipe Name

Cookbook Page

Recipe Name

Cookbook Page

Recipe Name

Cookbook Page

Recipe Name

Cookbook Page

Recipe Name

Cookbook Page

Recipe Name

Cookbook Page

Recipe Name

Cookbook Page

Recipe Name

Cookbook Page

Recipe Name

Cookbook Page

Recipe Name

Cookbook Page

Recipe Name

Cookbook Page

Recipe Name

Cookbook | Page

Recipe Name

Cookbook | Page

Recipe Name

Cookbook | Page

Recipe Name

Cookbook | Page

Recipe Name

Cookbook | Page

Recipe Name

Cookbook | Page

Recipe Name

Cookbook | Page

Recipe Name

Cookbook | Page

Recipe Name

Cookbook | Page

Recipe Name

Cookbook | Page

Recipe Name

Cookbook | Page

Recipe Name

Cookbook | Page

Recipe Name

Cookbook | Page

**Recipe Index**

Recipe Name

Cookbook | Page

Recipe Name

Cookbook | Page

Recipe Name

Cookbook | Page

Recipe Name

Cookbook | Page

Recipe Name

Cookbook | Page

Recipe Name

Cookbook | Page

Recipe Name

Cookbook | Page

Recipe Name

Cookbook | Page

Recipe Name

Cookbook | Page

Recipe Name

Cookbook | Page

Recipe Name

Cookbook | Page

Recipe Name

Cookbook | Page

Recipe Name

Cookbook | Page

# SALADS and SALAD DRESSINGS

Recipe Name

Cookbook | Page

Recipe Name

Cookbook | Page

Recipe Name

Cookbook | Page

Recipe Name

Cookbook | Page

Recipe Name

Cookbook | Page

Recipe Name

Cookbook | Page

Recipe Name

Cookbook | Page

Recipe Name

Cookbook | Page

Recipe Name

Cookbook | Page

Recipe Name

Cookbook | Page

Recipe Name

Cookbook | Page

Recipe Name

Cookbook | Page

Recipe Name

Cookbook | Page

**Recipe Index**

Recipe Name

Cookbook | Page

Recipe Name

Cookbook | Page

Recipe Name

Cookbook | Page

Recipe Name

Cookbook | Page

Recipe Name

Cookbook | Page

Recipe Name

Cookbook | Page

Recipe Name

Cookbook | Page

Recipe Name

Cookbook | Page

Recipe Name

Cookbook | Page

Recipe Name

Cookbook | Page

Recipe Name

Cookbook | Page

Recipe Name

Cookbook | Page

Recipe Name

Cookbook | Page

| Recipe Name | |
|---|---|
| Cookbook | Page |
| Recipe Name | |
| Cookbook | Page |
| Recipe Name | |
| Cookbook | Page |
| Recipe Name | |
| Cookbook | Page |
| Recipe Name | |
| Cookbook | Page |
| Recipe Name | |
| Cookbook | Page |
| Recipe Name | |
| Cookbook | Page |
| Recipe Name | |
| Cookbook | Page |
| Recipe Name | |
| Cookbook | Page |
| Recipe Name | |
| Cookbook | Page |
| Recipe Name | |
| Cookbook | Page |
| Recipe Name | |
| Cookbook | Page |
| Recipe Name | |
| Cookbook | Page |

## Recipe Index

| Recipe Name | |
|---|---|
| Cookbook | Page |
| Recipe Name | |
| Cookbook | Page |
| Recipe Name | |
| Cookbook | Page |
| Recipe Name | |
| Cookbook | Page |
| Recipe Name | |
| Cookbook | Page |
| Recipe Name | |
| Cookbook | Page |
| Recipe Name | |
| Cookbook | Page |
| Recipe Name | |
| Cookbook | Page |
| Recipe Name | |
| Cookbook | Page |
| Recipe Name | |
| Cookbook | Page |
| Recipe Name | |
| Cookbook | Page |
| Recipe Name | |
| Cookbook | Page |
| Recipe Name | |
| Cookbook | Page |

Recipe Name

Cookbook Page

Recipe Name

Cookbook Page

Recipe Name

Cookbook Page

Recipe Name

Cookbook Page

Recipe Name

Cookbook Page

Recipe Name

Cookbook Page

Recipe Name

Cookbook Page

Recipe Name

Cookbook Page

Recipe Name

Cookbook Page

Recipe Name

Cookbook Page

Recipe Name

Cookbook Page

Recipe Name

Cookbook Page

Recipe Name

Cookbook Page

**Recipe Index**

Recipe Name

Cookbook Page

Recipe Name

Cookbook Page

Recipe Name

Cookbook Page

Recipe Name

Cookbook Page

Recipe Name

Cookbook Page

Recipe Name

Cookbook Page

Recipe Name

Cookbook Page

Recipe Name

Cookbook Page

Recipe Name

Cookbook Page

Recipe Name

Cookbook Page

Recipe Name

Cookbook Page

Recipe Name

Cookbook Page

Recipe Name

Cookbook Page

Recipe Name

Cookbook | Page

Recipe Name

Cookbook | Page

Recipe Name

Cookbook | Page

Recipe Name

Cookbook | Page

Recipe Name

Cookbook | Page

Recipe Name

Cookbook | Page

Recipe Name

Cookbook | Page

Recipe Name

Cookbook | Page

Recipe Name

Cookbook | Page

Recipe Name

Cookbook | Page

Recipe Name

Cookbook | Page

Recipe Name

Cookbook | Page

Recipe Name

Cookbook | Page

**Recipe Index**

Recipe Name
Cookbook | Page

Recipe Name
Cookbook | Page

Recipe Name
Cookbook | Page

Recipe Name
Cookbook | Page

Recipe Name
Cookbook | Page

Recipe Name
Cookbook | Page

Recipe Name
Cookbook | Page

Recipe Name
Cookbook | Page

Recipe Name
Cookbook | Page

Recipe Name
Cookbook | Page

Recipe Name
Cookbook | Page

Recipe Name
Cookbook | Page

Recipe Name
Cookbook | Page

# VEGETABLES

Recipe Name Calico Beans

Cookbook Treasured recipes from Cornerstone Baptist Church Page 22

Recipe Name Calico Beans

Cookbook Nursing Delights Page 26

Recipe Name

Cookbook Page

Recipe Name Marinated Carrots

Cookbook Treasured Recipes - Cornerstone Church. Page 23

Recipe Name

Cookbook Page

Recipe Name

Cookbook Page

Recipe Name

Cookbook Page

Recipe Name

Cookbook Page

Recipe Name

Cookbook Page

Recipe Name

Cookbook Page

Recipe Name

Cookbook Page

Recipe Name

Cookbook Page

Recipe Name

Cookbook Page

**Recipe Index**

Recipe Name

Cookbook | Page

Recipe Name

Cookbook | Page

Recipe Name

Cookbook | Page

Recipe Name

Cookbook | Page

Recipe Name

Cookbook | Page

Recipe Name

Cookbook | Page

Recipe Name

Cookbook | Page

Recipe Name

Cookbook | Page

Recipe Name

Cookbook | Page

Recipe Name

Cookbook | Page

Recipe Name

Cookbook | Page

Recipe Name

Cookbook | Page

Recipe Name

Cookbook | Page

Recipe Name

Cookbook | Page

Recipe Name

Cookbook | Page

Recipe Name

Cookbook | Page

Recipe Name

Cookbook | Page

Recipe Name

Cookbook | Page

Recipe Name

Cookbook | Page

Recipe Name

Cookbook | Page

Recipe Name

Cookbook | Page

Recipe Name

Cookbook | Page

Recipe Name

Cookbook | Page

Recipe Name

Cookbook | Page

Recipe Name

Cookbook | Page

Recipe Name

Cookbook | Page

**Recipe Index**

Recipe Name
Cookbook Page

Recipe Name
Cookbook Page

Recipe Name
Cookbook Page

Recipe Name
Cookbook Page

Recipe Name
Cookbook Page

Recipe Name
Cookbook Page

Recipe Name
Cookbook Page

Recipe Name
Cookbook Page

Recipe Name
Cookbook Page

Recipe Name
Cookbook Page

Recipe Name
Cookbook Page

Recipe Name
Cookbook Page

Recipe Name
Cookbook Page

Recipe Name

Cookbook | Page

Recipe Name

Cookbook | Page

Recipe Name

Cookbook | Page

Recipe Name

Cookbook | Page

Recipe Name

Cookbook | Page

Recipe Name

Cookbook | Page

Recipe Name

Cookbook | Page

Recipe Name

Cookbook | Page

Recipe Name

Cookbook | Page

Recipe Name

Cookbook | Page

Recipe Name

Cookbook | Page

Recipe Name

Cookbook | Page

Recipe Name

Cookbook | Page

**Recipe Index**

Recipe Name

Cookbook Page

Recipe Name

Cookbook Page

Recipe Name

Cookbook Page

Recipe Name

Cookbook Page

Recipe Name

Cookbook Page

Recipe Name

Cookbook Page

Recipe Name

Cookbook Page

Recipe Name

Cookbook Page

Recipe Name

Cookbook Page

Recipe Name

Cookbook Page

Recipe Name

Cookbook Page

Recipe Name

Cookbook Page

Recipe Name

Cookbook Page

Recipe Name

Cookbook | Page

Recipe Name

Cookbook | Page

Recipe Name

Cookbook | Page

Recipe Name

Cookbook | Page

Recipe Name

Cookbook | Page

Recipe Name

Cookbook | Page

Recipe Name

Cookbook | Page

Recipe Name

Cookbook | Page

Recipe Name

Cookbook | Page

Recipe Name

Cookbook | Page

Recipe Name

Cookbook | Page

Recipe Name

Cookbook | Page

Recipe Name

Cookbook | Page

**Recipe Index**

Recipe Name

Cookbook | Page

Recipe Name

Cookbook | Page

Recipe Name

Cookbook | Page

Recipe Name

Cookbook | Page

Recipe Name

Cookbook | Page

Recipe Name

Cookbook | Page

Recipe Name

Cookbook | Page

Recipe Name

Cookbook | Page

Recipe Name

Cookbook | Page

Recipe Name

Cookbook | Page

Recipe Name

Cookbook | Page

Recipe Name

Cookbook | Page

Recipe Name

Cookbook | Page

# ENTRÉES POULTRY

Recipe Name

Cookbook | Page

Recipe Name

Cookbook | Page

Recipe Name

Cookbook | Page

Recipe Name

Cookbook | Page

Recipe Name

Cookbook | Page

Recipe Name

Cookbook | Page

Recipe Name

Cookbook | Page

Recipe Name

Cookbook | Page

Recipe Name

Cookbook | Page

Recipe Name

Cookbook | Page

Recipe Name

Cookbook | Page

Recipe Name

Cookbook | Page

Recipe Name

Cookbook | Page

## Recipe Index

Recipe Name

Cookbook | Page

Recipe Name

Cookbook | Page

Recipe Name

Cookbook | Page

Recipe Name

Cookbook | Page

Recipe Name

Cookbook | Page

Recipe Name

Cookbook | Page

Recipe Name

Cookbook | Page

Recipe Name

Cookbook | Page

Recipe Name

Cookbook | Page

Recipe Name

Cookbook | Page

Recipe Name

Cookbook | Page

Recipe Name

Cookbook | Page

Recipe Name

Cookbook | Page

Recipe Name

Cookbook | Page

Recipe Name

Cookbook | Page

Recipe Name

Cookbook | Page

Recipe Name

Cookbook | Page

Recipe Name

Cookbook | Page

Recipe Name

Cookbook | Page

Recipe Name

Cookbook | Page

Recipe Name

Cookbook | Page

Recipe Name

Cookbook | Page

Recipe Name

Cookbook | Page

Recipe Name

Cookbook | Page

Recipe Name

Cookbook | Page

Recipe Name

Cookbook | Page

**Recipe Index**

Recipe Name

Cookbook | Page

Recipe Name

Cookbook | Page

Recipe Name

Cookbook | Page

Recipe Name

Cookbook | Page

Recipe Name

Cookbook | Page

Recipe Name

Cookbook | Page

Recipe Name

Cookbook | Page

Recipe Name

Cookbook | Page

Recipe Name

Cookbook | Page

Recipe Name

Cookbook | Page

Recipe Name

Cookbook | Page

Recipe Name

Cookbook | Page

Recipe Name

Cookbook | Page

Recipe Name

Cookbook | Page

Recipe Name

Cookbook | Page

Recipe Name

Cookbook | Page

Recipe Name

Cookbook | Page

Recipe Name

Cookbook | Page

Recipe Name

Cookbook | Page

Recipe Name

Cookbook | Page

Recipe Name

Cookbook | Page

Recipe Name

Cookbook | Page

Recipe Name

Cookbook | Page

Recipe Name

Cookbook | Page

Recipe Name

Cookbook | Page

Recipe Name

Cookbook | Page

**Recipe Index**

| Recipe Name | |
|---|---|
| Cookbook | Page |
| Recipe Name | |
| Cookbook | Page |
| Recipe Name | |
| Cookbook | Page |
| Recipe Name | |
| Cookbook | Page |
| Recipe Name | |
| Cookbook | Page |
| Recipe Name | |
| Cookbook | Page |
| Recipe Name | |
| Cookbook | Page |
| Recipe Name | |
| Cookbook | Page |
| Recipe Name | |
| Cookbook | Page |
| Recipe Name | |
| Cookbook | Page |
| Recipe Name | |
| Cookbook | Page |
| Recipe Name | |
| Cookbook | Page |
| Recipe Name | |
| Cookbook | Page |

Recipe Name

Cookbook | Page

Recipe Name

Cookbook | Page

Recipe Name

Cookbook | Page

Recipe Name

Cookbook | Page

Recipe Name

Cookbook | Page

Recipe Name

Cookbook | Page

Recipe Name

Cookbook | Page

Recipe Name

Cookbook | Page

Recipe Name

Cookbook | Page

Recipe Name

Cookbook | Page

Recipe Name

Cookbook | Page

Recipe Name

Cookbook | Page

Recipe Name

Cookbook | Page

**Recipe Index**

Recipe Name

Cookbook | Page

Recipe Name

Cookbook | Page

Recipe Name

Cookbook | Page

Recipe Name

Cookbook | Page

Recipe Name

Cookbook | Page

Recipe Name

Cookbook | Page

Recipe Name

Cookbook | Page

Recipe Name

Cookbook | Page

Recipe Name

Cookbook | Page

Recipe Name

Cookbook | Page

Recipe Name

Cookbook | Page

Recipe Name

Cookbook | Page

Recipe Name

Cookbook | Page

# ENTRÉES MEAT

Recipe Name
Cookbook | Page

Recipe Name
Cookbook | Page

Recipe Name
Cookbook | Page

Recipe Name
Cookbook | Page

Recipe Name
Cookbook | Page

Recipe Name
Cookbook | Page

Recipe Name
Cookbook | Page

Recipe Name
Cookbook | Page

Recipe Name
Cookbook | Page

Recipe Name
Cookbook | Page

Recipe Name
Cookbook | Page

Recipe Name
Cookbook | Page

Recipe Name
Cookbook | Page

**Recipe Index**

Recipe Name

Cookbook | Page

Recipe Name

Cookbook | Page

Recipe Name

Cookbook | Page

Recipe Name

Cookbook | Page

Recipe Name

Cookbook | Page

Recipe Name

Cookbook | Page

Recipe Name

Cookbook | Page

Recipe Name

Cookbook | Page

Recipe Name

Cookbook | Page

Recipe Name

Cookbook | Page

Recipe Name

Cookbook | Page

Recipe Name

Cookbook | Page

Recipe Name

Cookbook | Page

Recipe Name

Cookbook | Page

Recipe Name

Cookbook | Page

Recipe Name

Cookbook | Page

Recipe Name

Cookbook | Page

Recipe Name

Cookbook | Page

Recipe Name

Cookbook | Page

Recipe Name

Cookbook | Page

Recipe Name

Cookbook | Page

Recipe Name

Cookbook | Page

Recipe Name

Cookbook | Page

Recipe Name

Cookbook | Page

Recipe Name

Cookbook | Page

Recipe Name

Cookbook | Page

**Recipe Index**

Recipe Name

Cookbook Page

Recipe Name

Cookbook Page

Recipe Name

Cookbook Page

Recipe Name

Cookbook Page

Recipe Name

Cookbook Page

Recipe Name

Cookbook Page

Recipe Name

Cookbook Page

Recipe Name

Cookbook Page

Recipe Name

Cookbook Page

Recipe Name

Cookbook Page

Recipe Name

Cookbook Page

Recipe Name

Cookbook Page

Recipe Name

Cookbook Page

Recipe Name

Cookbook | Page

Recipe Name

Cookbook | Page

Recipe Name

Cookbook | Page

Recipe Name

Cookbook | Page

Recipe Name

Cookbook | Page

Recipe Name

Cookbook | Page

Recipe Name

Cookbook | Page

Recipe Name

Cookbook | Page

Recipe Name

Cookbook | Page

Recipe Name

Cookbook | Page

Recipe Name

Cookbook | Page

Recipe Name

Cookbook | Page

Recipe Name

Cookbook | Page

**Recipe Index**

Recipe Name

Cookbook | Page

Recipe Name

Cookbook | Page

Recipe Name

Cookbook | Page

Recipe Name

Cookbook | Page

Recipe Name

Cookbook | Page

Recipe Name

Cookbook | Page

Recipe Name

Cookbook | Page

Recipe Name

Cookbook | Page

Recipe Name

Cookbook | Page

Recipe Name

Cookbook | Page

Recipe Name

Cookbook | Page

Recipe Name

Cookbook | Page

Recipe Name

Cookbook | Page

Recipe Name

Cookbook | Page

Recipe Name

Cookbook | Page

Recipe Name

Cookbook | Page

Recipe Name

Cookbook | Page

Recipe Name

Cookbook | Page

Recipe Name

Cookbook | Page

Recipe Name

Cookbook | Page

Recipe Name

Cookbook | Page

Recipe Name

Cookbook | Page

Recipe Name

Cookbook | Page

Recipe Name

Cookbook | Page

Recipe Name

Cookbook | Page

Recipe Name

Cookbook | Page

**Recipe Index**

Recipe Name

Cookbook | Page

Recipe Name

Cookbook | Page

Recipe Name

Cookbook | Page

Recipe Name

Cookbook | Page

Recipe Name

Cookbook | Page

Recipe Name

Cookbook | Page

Recipe Name

Cookbook | Page

Recipe Name

Cookbook | Page

Recipe Name

Cookbook | Page

Recipe Name

Cookbook | Page

Recipe Name

Cookbook | Page

Recipe Name

Cookbook | Page

Recipe Name

Cookbook | Page

# ENTRÉES SEAFOOD

Recipe Name

Cookbook | Page

Recipe Name

Cookbook | Page

Recipe Name

Cookbook | Page

Recipe Name

Cookbook | Page

Recipe Name

Cookbook | Page

Recipe Name

Cookbook | Page

Recipe Name

Cookbook | Page

Recipe Name

Cookbook | Page

Recipe Name

Cookbook | Page

Recipe Name

Cookbook | Page

Recipe Name

Cookbook | Page

Recipe Name

Cookbook | Page

Recipe Name

Cookbook | Page

**Recipe Index**

Recipe Name

Cookbook | Page

Recipe Name

Cookbook | Page

Recipe Name

Cookbook | Page

Recipe Name

Cookbook | Page

Recipe Name

Cookbook | Page

Recipe Name

Cookbook | Page

Recipe Name

Cookbook | Page

Recipe Name

Cookbook | Page

Recipe Name

Cookbook | Page

Recipe Name

Cookbook | Page

Recipe Name

Cookbook | Page

Recipe Name

Cookbook | Page

Recipe Name

Cookbook | Page

Recipe Name

Cookbook | Page

Recipe Name

Cookbook | Page

Recipe Name

Cookbook | Page

Recipe Name

Cookbook | Page

Recipe Name

Cookbook | Page

Recipe Name

Cookbook | Page

Recipe Name

Cookbook | Page

Recipe Name

Cookbook | Page

Recipe Name

Cookbook | Page

Recipe Name

Cookbook | Page

Recipe Name

Cookbook | Page

Recipe Name

Cookbook | Page

Recipe Name

Cookbook | Page

**Recipe Index**

Recipe Name

Cookbook | Page

Recipe Name

Cookbook | Page

Recipe Name

Cookbook | Page

Recipe Name

Cookbook | Page

Recipe Name

Cookbook | Page

Recipe Name

Cookbook | Page

Recipe Name

Cookbook | Page

Recipe Name

Cookbook | Page

Recipe Name

Cookbook | Page

Recipe Name

Cookbook | Page

Recipe Name

Cookbook | Page

Recipe Name

Cookbook | Page

Recipe Name

Cookbook | Page

Recipe Name

Cookbook | Page

Recipe Name

Cookbook | Page

Recipe Name

Cookbook | Page

Recipe Name

Cookbook | Page

Recipe Name

Cookbook | Page

Recipe Name

Cookbook | Page

Recipe Name

Cookbook | Page

Recipe Name

Cookbook | Page

Recipe Name

Cookbook | Page

Recipe Name

Cookbook | Page

Recipe Name

Cookbook | Page

Recipe Name

Cookbook | Page

Recipe Name

Cookbook | Page

**Recipe Index**

Recipe Name

Cookbook | Page

Recipe Name

Cookbook | Page

Recipe Name

Cookbook | Page

Recipe Name

Cookbook | Page

Recipe Name

Cookbook | Page

Recipe Name

Cookbook | Page

Recipe Name

Cookbook | Page

Recipe Name

Cookbook | Page

Recipe Name

Cookbook | Page

Recipe Name

Cookbook | Page

Recipe Name

Cookbook | Page

Recipe Name

Cookbook | Page

Recipe Name

Cookbook | Page

Recipe Name

Cookbook | Page

Recipe Name

Cookbook | Page

Recipe Name

Cookbook | Page

Recipe Name

Cookbook | Page

Recipe Name

Cookbook | Page

Recipe Name

Cookbook | Page

Recipe Name

Cookbook | Page

Recipe Name

Cookbook | Page

Recipe Name

Cookbook | Page

Recipe Name

Cookbook | Page

Recipe Name

Cookbook | Page

Recipe Name

Cookbook | Page

Recipe Name

Cookbook | Page

**Recipe Index**

Recipe Name

Cookbook | Page

Recipe Name

Cookbook | Page

Recipe Name

Cookbook | Page

Recipe Name

Cookbook | Page

Recipe Name

Cookbook | Page

Recipe Name

Cookbook | Page

Recipe Name

Cookbook | Page

Recipe Name

Cookbook | Page

Recipe Name

Cookbook | Page

Recipe Name

Cookbook | Page

Recipe Name

Cookbook | Page

Recipe Name

Cookbook | Page

Recipe Name

Cookbook | Page

# ENTRÉES
# CASSEROLES

Recipe Name *Shipwreck*

Cookbook *Grandma's Cooking* Page *128*

Recipe Name

Cookbook Page

Recipe Name

Cookbook Page

Recipe Name

Cookbook Page

Recipe Name

Cookbook Page

Recipe Name

Cookbook Page

Recipe Name

Cookbook Page

Recipe Name

Cookbook Page

Recipe Name

Cookbook Page

Recipe Name

Cookbook Page

Recipe Name

Cookbook Page

Recipe Name

Cookbook Page

Recipe Name

Cookbook Page

**Recipe Index**

| Recipe Name | |
|---|---|
| Cookbook | Page |
| Recipe Name | |
| Cookbook | Page |
| Recipe Name | |
| Cookbook | Page |
| Recipe Name | |
| Cookbook | Page |
| Recipe Name | |
| Cookbook | Page |
| Recipe Name | |
| Cookbook | Page |
| Recipe Name | |
| Cookbook | Page |
| Recipe Name | |
| Cookbook | Page |
| Recipe Name | |
| Cookbook | Page |
| Recipe Name | |
| Cookbook | Page |
| Recipe Name | |
| Cookbook | Page |
| Recipe Name | |
| Cookbook | Page |
| Recipe Name | |
| Cookbook | Page |

Recipe Name
Cookbook Page

Recipe Name
Cookbook Page

Recipe Name
Cookbook Page

Recipe Name
Cookbook Page

Recipe Name
Cookbook Page

Recipe Name
Cookbook Page

Recipe Name
Cookbook Page

Recipe Name
Cookbook Page

Recipe Name
Cookbook Page

Recipe Name
Cookbook Page

Recipe Name
Cookbook Page

Recipe Name
Cookbook Page

Recipe Name
Cookbook Page

**Recipe Index**

Recipe Name

Cookbook | Page

Recipe Name

Cookbook | Page

Recipe Name

Cookbook | Page

Recipe Name

Cookbook | Page

Recipe Name

Cookbook | Page

Recipe Name

Cookbook | Page

Recipe Name

Cookbook | Page

Recipe Name

Cookbook | Page

Recipe Name

Cookbook | Page

Recipe Name

Cookbook | Page

Recipe Name

Cookbook | Page

Recipe Name

Cookbook | Page

Recipe Name

Cookbook | Page

Recipe Name

Cookbook | Page

Recipe Name

Cookbook | Page

Recipe Name

Cookbook | Page

Recipe Name

Cookbook | Page

Recipe Name

Cookbook | Page

Recipe Name

Cookbook | Page

Recipe Name

Cookbook | Page

Recipe Name

Cookbook | Page

Recipe Name

Cookbook | Page

Recipe Name

Cookbook | Page

Recipe Name

Cookbook | Page

Recipe Name

Cookbook | Page

Recipe Name

Cookbook | Page

**Recipe Index**

Recipe Name
Cookbook | Page

Recipe Name
Cookbook | Page

Recipe Name
Cookbook | Page

Recipe Name
Cookbook | Page

Recipe Name
Cookbook | Page

Recipe Name
Cookbook | Page

Recipe Name
Cookbook | Page

Recipe Name
Cookbook | Page

Recipe Name
Cookbook | Page

Recipe Name
Cookbook | Page

Recipe Name
Cookbook | Page

Recipe Name
Cookbook | Page

Recipe Name
Cookbook | Page

Recipe Name

Cookbook | Page

Recipe Name

Cookbook | Page

Recipe Name

Cookbook | Page

Recipe Name

Cookbook | Page

Recipe Name

Cookbook | Page

Recipe Name

Cookbook | Page

Recipe Name

Cookbook | Page

Recipe Name

Cookbook | Page

Recipe Name

Cookbook | Page

Recipe Name

Cookbook | Page

Recipe Name

Cookbook | Page

Recipe Name

Cookbook | Page

Recipe Name

Cookbook | Page

**Recipe Index**

Recipe Name

Cookbook | Page

Recipe Name

Cookbook | Page

Recipe Name

Cookbook | Page

Recipe Name

Cookbook | Page

Recipe Name

Cookbook | Page

Recipe Name

Cookbook | Page

Recipe Name

Cookbook | Page

Recipe Name

Cookbook | Page

Recipe Name

Cookbook | Page

Recipe Name

Cookbook | Page

Recipe Name

Cookbook | Page

Recipe Name

Cookbook | Page

Recipe Name

Cookbook | Page

# DESSERTS, PIES and PASTRIES

Recipe Name Peach Ice Cream

Cookbook Our Best Recipes (S.L.) Page 131

Recipe Name Banana Pudding

Cookbook Our Best Recipes (S.L.) Page 139

Recipe Name

Cookbook Page

Recipe Name Peach Cobbler (yellow P.V.)

Cookbook Our Faborite Recipes Page 68

Recipe Name Peach Cobbler (Brown)

Cookbook Recipes from our Best Cooks Page 72

Recipe Name

Cookbook Page

Recipe Name Bread Pudding & sauce 26-27

Cookbook Heavenly Delights (Jody's) Page

Recipe Name

Cookbook Page

Recipe Name

Cookbook Page

Recipe Name

Cookbook Page

Recipe Name

Cookbook Page

Recipe Name

Cookbook Page

Recipe Name

Cookbook Page

**Recipe Index**

Recipe Name

Cookbook | Page

Recipe Name

Cookbook | Page

Recipe Name

Cookbook | Page

Recipe Name

Cookbook | Page

Recipe Name

Cookbook | Page

Recipe Name

Cookbook | Page

Recipe Name

Cookbook | Page

Recipe Name

Cookbook | Page

Recipe Name

Cookbook | Page

Recipe Name

Cookbook | Page

Recipe Name

Cookbook | Page

Recipe Name

Cookbook | Page

Recipe Name

Cookbook | Page

Recipe Name

Cookbook | Page

Recipe Name

Cookbook | Page

Recipe Name

Cookbook | Page

Recipe Name

Cookbook | Page

Recipe Name

Cookbook | Page

Recipe Name

Cookbook | Page

Recipe Name

Cookbook | Page

Recipe Name

Cookbook | Page

Recipe Name

Cookbook | Page

Recipe Name

Cookbook | Page

Recipe Name

Cookbook | Page

Recipe Name

Cookbook | Page

Recipe Name

Cookbook | Page

**Recipe Index**

Recipe Name

Cookbook | Page

Recipe Name

Cookbook | Page

Recipe Name

Cookbook | Page

Recipe Name

Cookbook | Page

Recipe Name

Cookbook | Page

Recipe Name

Cookbook | Page

Recipe Name

Cookbook | Page

Recipe Name

Cookbook | Page

Recipe Name

Cookbook | Page

Recipe Name

Cookbook | Page

Recipe Name

Cookbook | Page

Recipe Name

Cookbook | Page

Recipe Name

Cookbook | Page

Recipe Name

Cookbook | Page

Recipe Name

Cookbook | Page

Recipe Name

Cookbook | Page

Recipe Name

Cookbook | Page

Recipe Name

Cookbook | Page

Recipe Name

Cookbook | Page

Recipe Name

Cookbook | Page

Recipe Name

Cookbook | Page

Recipe Name

Cookbook | Page

Recipe Name

Cookbook | Page

Recipe Name

Cookbook | Page

Recipe Name

Cookbook | Page

Recipe Name

Cookbook | Page

## Recipe Index

| Recipe Name | |
|---|---|
| Cookbook | Page |
| Recipe Name | |
| Cookbook | Page |
| Recipe Name | |
| Cookbook | Page |
| Recipe Name | |
| Cookbook | Page |
| Recipe Name | |
| Cookbook | Page |
| Recipe Name | |
| Cookbook | Page |
| Recipe Name | |
| Cookbook | Page |
| Recipe Name | |
| Cookbook | Page |
| Recipe Name | |
| Cookbook | Page |
| Recipe Name | |
| Cookbook | Page |
| Recipe Name | |
| Cookbook | Page |
| Recipe Name | |
| Cookbook | Page |
| Recipe Name | |
| Cookbook | Page |

| Recipe Name | |
|---|---|
| Cookbook | Page |
| Recipe Name | |
| Cookbook | Page |
| Recipe Name | |
| Cookbook | Page |
| Recipe Name | |
| Cookbook | Page |
| Recipe Name | |
| Cookbook | Page |
| Recipe Name | |
| Cookbook | Page |
| Recipe Name | |
| Cookbook | Page |
| Recipe Name | |
| Cookbook | Page |
| Recipe Name | |
| Cookbook | Page |
| Recipe Name | |
| Cookbook | Page |
| Recipe Name | |
| Cookbook | Page |
| Recipe Name | |
| Cookbook | Page |
| Recipe Name | |
| Cookbook | Page |

**Recipe Index**

| Recipe Name | |
|---|---|
| Cookbook | Page |
| Recipe Name | |
| Cookbook | Page |
| Recipe Name | |
| Cookbook | Page |
| Recipe Name | |
| Cookbook | Page |
| Recipe Name | |
| Cookbook | Page |
| Recipe Name | |
| Cookbook | Page |
| Recipe Name | |
| Cookbook | Page |
| Recipe Name | |
| Cookbook | Page |
| Recipe Name | |
| Cookbook | Page |
| Recipe Name | |
| Cookbook | Page |
| Recipe Name | |
| Cookbook | Page |
| Recipe Name | |
| Cookbook | Page |
| Recipe Name | |
| Cookbook | Page |

# CAKES, FROSTINGS and FILLINGS

Recipe Name White Chocolate Cake

Cookbook Our Best Recipes (S.L.) Page 57

Recipe Name

Cookbook Page

Recipe Name

Cookbook Page

Recipe Name

Cookbook Page

Recipe Name

Cookbook Page

Recipe Name

Cookbook Page

Recipe Name

Cookbook Page

Recipe Name

Cookbook Page

Recipe Name

Cookbook Page

Recipe Name

Cookbook Page

Recipe Name

Cookbook Page

Recipe Name

Cookbook Page

Recipe Name

Cookbook Page

## Recipe Index

Recipe Name

Cookbook | Page

Recipe Name

Cookbook | Page

Recipe Name

Cookbook | Page

Recipe Name

Cookbook | Page

Recipe Name

Cookbook | Page

Recipe Name

Cookbook | Page

Recipe Name

Cookbook | Page

Recipe Name

Cookbook | Page

Recipe Name

Cookbook | Page

Recipe Name

Cookbook | Page

Recipe Name

Cookbook | Page

Recipe Name

Cookbook | Page

Recipe Name

Cookbook | Page

Recipe Name

Cookbook Page

Recipe Name

Cookbook Page

Recipe Name

Cookbook Page

Recipe Name

Cookbook Page

Recipe Name

Cookbook Page

Recipe Name

Cookbook Page

Recipe Name

Cookbook Page

Recipe Name

Cookbook Page

Recipe Name

Cookbook Page

Recipe Name

Cookbook Page

Recipe Name

Cookbook Page

Recipe Name

Cookbook Page

Recipe Name

Cookbook Page

**Recipe Index**

Recipe Name

Cookbook | Page

Recipe Name

Cookbook | Page

Recipe Name

Cookbook | Page

Recipe Name

Cookbook | Page

Recipe Name

Cookbook | Page

Recipe Name

Cookbook | Page

Recipe Name

Cookbook | Page

Recipe Name

Cookbook | Page

Recipe Name

Cookbook | Page

Recipe Name

Cookbook | Page

Recipe Name

Cookbook | Page

Recipe Name

Cookbook | Page

Recipe Name

Cookbook | Page

Recipe Name

Cookbook | Page

Recipe Name

Cookbook | Page

Recipe Name

Cookbook | Page

Recipe Name

Cookbook | Page

Recipe Name

Cookbook | Page

Recipe Name

Cookbook | Page

Recipe Name

Cookbook | Page

Recipe Name

Cookbook | Page

Recipe Name

Cookbook | Page

Recipe Name

Cookbook | Page

Recipe Name

Cookbook | Page

Recipe Name

Cookbook | Page

Recipe Name

Cookbook | Page

**Recipe Index**

Recipe Name

Cookbook | Page

Recipe Name

Cookbook | Page

Recipe Name

Cookbook | Page

Recipe Name

Cookbook | Page

Recipe Name

Cookbook | Page

Recipe Name

Cookbook | Page

Recipe Name

Cookbook | Page

Recipe Name

Cookbook | Page

Recipe Name

Cookbook | Page

Recipe Name

Cookbook | Page

Recipe Name

Cookbook | Page

Recipe Name

Cookbook | Page

Recipe Name

Cookbook | Page

Recipe Name

Cookbook | Page

Recipe Name

Cookbook | Page

Recipe Name

Cookbook | Page

Recipe Name

Cookbook | Page

Recipe Name

Cookbook | Page

Recipe Name

Cookbook | Page

Recipe Name

Cookbook | Page

Recipe Name

Cookbook | Page

Recipe Name

Cookbook | Page

Recipe Name

Cookbook | Page

Recipe Name

Cookbook | Page

Recipe Name

Cookbook | Page

Recipe Name

Cookbook | Page

**Recipe Index**

Recipe Name

Cookbook | Page

Recipe Name

Cookbook | Page

Recipe Name

Cookbook | Page

Recipe Name

Cookbook | Page

Recipe Name

Cookbook | Page

Recipe Name

Cookbook | Page

Recipe Name

Cookbook | Page

Recipe Name

Cookbook | Page

Recipe Name

Cookbook | Page

Recipe Name

Cookbook | Page

Recipe Name

Cookbook | Page

Recipe Name

Cookbook | Page

Recipe Name

Cookbook | Page

# COOKIES

| Recipe Name | Cookbook | Page |
|---|---|---|
| Peanut Blossoms | Our Best Recipes (S.L.) | 127 |
| | | |
| | | |
| | | |
| | | |
| | | |
| | | |
| | | |
| | | |
| | | |
| Rice Krispie Treats | Cooking w/ Love & Cereal | 115 |
| | | |
| | | |

## Recipe Index

Recipe Name

Cookbook | Page

Recipe Name

Cookbook | Page

Recipe Name

Cookbook | Page

Recipe Name

Cookbook | Page

Recipe Name

Cookbook | Page

Recipe Name

Cookbook | Page

Recipe Name

Cookbook | Page

Recipe Name

Cookbook | Page

Recipe Name

Cookbook | Page

Recipe Name

Cookbook | Page

Recipe Name

Cookbook | Page

Recipe Name

Cookbook | Page

Recipe Name

Cookbook | Page

Recipe Name

Cookbook | Page

Recipe Name

Cookbook | Page

Recipe Name

Cookbook | Page

Recipe Name

Cookbook | Page

Recipe Name

Cookbook | Page

Recipe Name

Cookbook | Page

Recipe Name

Cookbook | Page

Recipe Name

Cookbook | Page

Recipe Name

Cookbook | Page

Recipe Name

Cookbook | Page

Recipe Name

Cookbook | Page

Recipe Name

Cookbook | Page

Recipe Name

Cookbook | Page

**Recipe Index**

Recipe Name

Cookbook | Page

Recipe Name

Cookbook | Page

Recipe Name

Cookbook | Page

Recipe Name

Cookbook | Page

Recipe Name

Cookbook | Page

Recipe Name

Cookbook | Page

Recipe Name

Cookbook | Page

Recipe Name

Cookbook | Page

Recipe Name

Cookbook | Page

Recipe Name

Cookbook | Page

Recipe Name

Cookbook | Page

Recipe Name

Cookbook | Page

Recipe Name

Cookbook | Page

Recipe Name

Cookbook | Page

Recipe Name

Cookbook | Page

Recipe Name

Cookbook | Page

Recipe Name

Cookbook | Page

Recipe Name

Cookbook | Page

Recipe Name

Cookbook | Page

Recipe Name

Cookbook | Page

Recipe Name

Cookbook | Page

Recipe Name

Cookbook | Page

Recipe Name

Cookbook | Page

Recipe Name

Cookbook | Page

Recipe Name

Cookbook | Page

Recipe Name

Cookbook | Page

**Recipe Index**

Recipe Name

Cookbook | Page

Recipe Name

Cookbook | Page

Recipe Name

Cookbook | Page

Recipe Name

Cookbook | Page

Recipe Name

Cookbook | Page

Recipe Name

Cookbook | Page

Recipe Name

Cookbook | Page

Recipe Name

Cookbook | Page

Recipe Name

Cookbook | Page

Recipe Name

Cookbook | Page

Recipe Name

Cookbook | Page

Recipe Name

Cookbook | Page

Recipe Name

Cookbook | Page

Recipe Name

Cookbook | Page

Recipe Name

Cookbook | Page

Recipe Name

Cookbook | Page

Recipe Name

Cookbook | Page

Recipe Name

Cookbook | Page

Recipe Name

Cookbook | Page

Recipe Name

Cookbook | Page

Recipe Name

Cookbook | Page

Recipe Name

Cookbook | Page

Recipe Name

Cookbook | Page

Recipe Name

Cookbook | Page

Recipe Name

Cookbook | Page

Recipe Name

Cookbook | Page

**Recipe Index**

Recipe Name

Cookbook | Page

Recipe Name

Cookbook | Page

Recipe Name

Cookbook | Page

Recipe Name

Cookbook | Page

Recipe Name

Cookbook | Page

Recipe Name

Cookbook | Page

Recipe Name

Cookbook | Page

Recipe Name

Cookbook | Page

Recipe Name

Cookbook | Page

Recipe Name

Cookbook | Page

Recipe Name

Cookbook | Page

Recipe Name

Cookbook | Page

Recipe Name

Cookbook | Page

# CANDIES

Recipe Name

Cookbook | Page

Recipe Name

Cookbook | Page

Recipe Name

Cookbook | Page

Recipe Name

Cookbook | Page

Recipe Name

Cookbook | Page

Recipe Name

Cookbook | Page

Recipe Name

Cookbook | Page

Recipe Name

Cookbook | Page

Recipe Name

Cookbook | Page

Recipe Name

Cookbook | Page

Recipe Name

Cookbook | Page

Recipe Name

Cookbook | Page

Recipe Name

Cookbook | Page

**Recipe Index**

Recipe Name

Cookbook | Page

Recipe Name

Cookbook | Page

Recipe Name

Cookbook | Page

Recipe Name

Cookbook | Page

Recipe Name

Cookbook | Page

Recipe Name

Cookbook | Page

Recipe Name

Cookbook | Page

Recipe Name

Cookbook | Page

Recipe Name

Cookbook | Page

Recipe Name

Cookbook | Page

Recipe Name

Cookbook | Page

Recipe Name

Cookbook | Page

Recipe Name

Cookbook | Page

To order your "Recipe Index for cookbook collectors," send check or money order to:

**MARIA BAKER**
**9 NARVAEZ WAY**
**HOT SPRINGS VILLAGE, AR 71909**

Please send ______ copies of "Recipe Index for cookbook collectors" at $12.95 each plus $2.50 postage and handling per book. For Arkansas delivery add $.84 sales tax per book. Make checks payable to Maria Baker, 9 Narvaez Way, Hot Springs Village, AR 71909.

NAME ........................................

STREET ........................................

CITY ........................................

STATE ........................ ZIP ............

Recipe Index for cookbook collectors

. . . . Finally, at your fingertips . . .

Your favorite recipes from your cookbook collection!

To order your "Recipe Index for cookbook collectors," send check or money order to:

**MARIA BAKER**
**9 NARVAEZ WAY**
**HOT SPRINGS VILLAGE, AR 71909**

Please send ______ copies of "Recipe Index for cookbook collectors" at $12.95 each plus $2.50 postage and handling per book. For Arkansas delivery add $.84 sales tax per book. Make checks payable to Maria Baker, 9 Narvaez Way, Hot Springs Village, AR 71909.

NAME ........................................

STREET ........................................

CITY ........................................

STATE ........................ ZIP ............

Recipe Index for cookbook collectors

. . . . Finally, at your fingertips . . .

Your favorite recipes from your cookbook collection!

To order your "Recipe Index for cookbook collectors," send check or money order to:

**MARIA BAKER**
**9 NARVAEZ WAY**
**HOT SPRINGS VILLAGE, AR 71909**

Please send ______ copies of "Recipe Index for cookbook collectors" at $12.95 each plus $2.50 postage and handling per book. For Arkansas delivery add $.84 sales tax per book. Make checks payable to Maria Baker, 9 Narvaez Way, Hot Springs Village, AR 71909.

NAME ........................................

STREET ........................................

CITY ........................................

STATE ........................ ZIP ............